The Family Tree

Story by Julie Ellis
Illustrations by Meredith Thomas

Nathan struggled through the front door,
carrying a big box.
"Help me with this, please, Tess,"
he gasped. "It's really heavy!"

"Be careful! Don't drop it!"
warned his sister, as she rushed over
to grab the box.
"We mustn't break anything.
Grandma's unhappy enough already."

Nathan and Tess and their parents
were helping Grandma to move into a new house.
But Grandma was upset.
She thought the new house was too small,
and it didn't feel like home.

"What's in here anyway?" asked Tess,
as they put the box down carefully.

Nathan opened it and peered inside.
"It's full of photos," he said,
and he pulled one out.

It was a photo of a baby.
The writing on the back said:

John, six months old

"Guess who this is?" grinned Nathan,
as he held up the photo.
"It's Dad when he was a baby!"

Tess laughed.
"That baby doesn't look much like Dad. He has no teeth and no hair!" she said.

Grandma came into the room.

"Where do you want me
to put these photos?" Nathan asked her.

Grandma looked tired.
"I'd like them where I can see them,"
she replied, "but I don't have much room
in this house."
She pointed to a cupboard.
"Perhaps the albums could go in there.
I don't know where to put that box."

Nathan put the albums away,
then he looked at the other photos.
They were in a bit of a mess,
and some of them were old and bent.

"Grandma, could we take these photos home and have a good look at them?" asked Nathan.

"We might find some more photos of Dad when he was little," laughed Tess.

"Yes, of course you can," answered Grandma.

"You two can go home now with Dad, while I stay here with Grandma," said Mom. "She's very tired and I want to help her finish unpacking."

When the children arrived home,
they spread the photos out on the floor
and looked at them together.

"I have an idea," said Tess.
"We could use these photos
to make a family tree.
If we scanned the photos into the computer,
we could make the tree look special."

Tess helped Nathan find the best photo
of each person in Grandma's family.
Then she put them into four rows
to see how the tree would look.

In the first row,
she placed an old, faded photo
of Grandma's mother and father.
In the second row,
she put a black and white wedding portrait
of Grandma and Grandpa.

Underneath the portrait,
she placed two more old photos.
One was of Dad's sister and Grandpa,
and the other was of Dad.
In the last row were photos
of Tess and Nathan, and their cousin Emily.

"Now let's scan them into the computer,"
said Tess to Nathan.

They gathered up the photos
and took them to the computer.
Using the scanner, Tess copied each photo
onto the screen and added the names.

"It's getting late," she said to Nathan,
"and we still have to decide on a border.
We'll finish it tomorrow."

After school the next day,
Nathan hurried home.
He wanted to surprise Tess
by adding the border himself.

He turned on the computer
and pressed some keys.
Where were the photos?
They weren't coming up on the screen!

Nathan felt sick.
Had he deleted the files by mistake?
What would Tess say?

But when Tess saw what Nathan had done,
she wasn't worried.
"Guess what I remembered to do last night,"
she said. "I made a back-up file."

Tess opened the file,
and they looked at the photos again.
Then they decided on a border,
and Tess showed Nathan
how to place it around the edge.

"This looks good, Tess," said Nathan,
as he watched the page being printed out.
"Let's show Dad."

Dad thought they had done a great job.
"It just needs one more thing," he said.
"If we put it in a frame,
Grandma could hang it on her wall."

Dad took them to a shop
where Nathan chose a gold frame.
Now the family tree looked perfect.

When Grandma saw it, she smiled
and hugged the children.
"I love it," she said.
"This is just what I need
to make this house feel like home."